# INTRODUCTION

*D*id you know that a snake breathes through only one lung, which can be three-quarters as long as its body? Or that desert toads survive ten months of drought sealed in underground tombs, breathing only through their skin?

Are you aware that there are lizard species that are all-female, with the ability to "clone" themselves without mating with males? Or that a horned lizard squirts blood from its eyes to startle predators?

You'll meet these and many other fascinating snakes, lizards, toads, frogs, and turtles in *50 Common Reptiles and Amphibians of the Southwest*.

Still a little squeamish about slithery snakes and slippery toads? Fear of reptiles and their kin is a learned, not instinctive, behavior—an infant watching a snake will giggle with delight, not recoil in horror. So the more we learn about reptiles and amphibians, the closer we can come to understanding and then enjoying them. Furthermore, to paraphrase the great ecologist Edward O. Wilson, the more we learn about the workings of the natural world, the more we appreciate ourselves and our role therein.

## WHAT ARE REPTILES AND AMPHIBIANS?

Cecil R. Schwalbe

It's easy to oversimplify the differences between reptiles and amphibians. You could say that reptiles are scaly and amphibians are slimy, but what about soft-shelled turtles, which are reptiles? You could say that reptiles live on land and amphibians stay near water, but besides turtles there are snakes that spend virtually their entire lives in water, and toads that live in deserts. So we have to get a little more technical in our distinction.

Virtually all amphibians must reproduce in water—their eggs have no shells and would quickly dry out if exposed to air. The newly hatched amphibian is usually a larval stage—for example, the tadpole of frogs and toads—that breathes through gills and gradually develops limbs and lungs that enable it to emerge onto dry land. However, the skin of amphibians remains moist and permeable to air; in fact, amphibians breathe through their skin as well as their lungs. So amphibians must either stay near water or *estivate* underground during dry periods to prevent fatal water loss through the skin. Amphibians of the Southwest include salamanders, toads, and frogs.

In contrast, reptiles reproduce on land. Depending on the species, they can produce eggs, which have a leathery covering to prevent drying out, or live young, which are immediately able to fend for themselves. There is no larval stage—baby reptiles look like miniature versions of their parents. Reptiles have dry, scaly skin that is thirty times more resistant to desiccation than amphibian skin, so some reptiles can withstand truly desert conditions. Southwestern reptiles include turtles, tortoises, lizards, and snakes.

## ENJOYING REPTILES AND AMPHIBIANS IN THE SOUTHWEST

The best time to see reptiles and amphibians in the Southwest is spring through fall, although it is possible to see them out sunning or hunting during any month. Remember that even the most abundant kinds of reptiles and amphibians are well camouflaged—and thus can be challenging to spot. The best way to find them is the best way to find other animals, too—walk slowly and quietly, and look carefully.

A particularly good time to look for reptiles and amphibians is on a summer evening after a good rain. Roadside ditches where runoff collects are great amphibian hangouts, while snakes prefer—often to their misfortune—stretching out on a warm, smooth surface such as road asphalt.

For daytime viewing, wait until the air temperature is warm but not too warm. Generally, in hot weather reptiles and amphibians will be active in early morning and late afternoon. In more temperate weather, they will wait

# 50

# COMMON REPTILES & AMPHIBIANS

## OF THE SOUTHWEST

Jonathan Hanson *and* Roseann Beggy Hanson

WESTERN NATIONAL PARKS ASSOCIATION
TUCSON, ARIZONA

**WARNING**: *You should never touch or even closely approach any of the animals listed in this book. If you do the animal may defend itself and bite or otherwise injure you. The publisher and authors accept no liability for any injuries or damages you may receive while acting upon or using the contents of this publication.*

ACKNOWLEDGMENTS

The authors thank members of the Tucson Herpetological Society David L. Hardy, Sr., Roger Repp, and Allison Titcomb for their reviews of initial species lists and final manuscript. Their excellent comments and wide knowledge of the herpetofauna of the Southwest were invaluable. Phil Rosen also offered valuable information, and Derek Gallagher of Western National Parks Association provided keen editing as well as natural history knowledge.

Library of Congress Cataloging-in-Publication Data
Hanson, Jonathan.
    50 common reptiles & amphibians of the Southwest / Jonathan Hanson
  and Roseann Beggy Hanson.
        p.   cm.
  Includes bibliographical references and index.
  ISBN 1-877856-81-9 (pbk.)
  1. Reptiles — Southwest, New. 2. Amphibians — Southwest, New.
I. Hanson, Roseann Beggy.    II. Title.
QL653.S68H35    1997
597.9'0979 - dc21

                                           97-22148
                                           CIP

Published by Western National Parks Association

The net proceeds from WNPA publications support educational and research programs in your national parks.

Editorial: Derek Gallagher
Design: Campana Design
Illustration: Barbara Terkanian
Printing: Sung In
Printed in Korea
Cover photograph: Larry Lindahl

until the sun warms up a bit—usually more than sixty-five degrees Fahrenheit.

Reptiles and amphibians can be hard to see for more than a second—sometimes all we get is a fleeting glimpse as they slip away into the undergrowth or dive into a pond. Binoculars can be a handy remedy for getting close without getting too close. They don't have to be fancy, expensive ones—just good enough to offer a clear view. Seven- to eight-power magnification works well for all-purpose field observation.

For excellent opportunities to see reptiles and amphibians, and many other plants and animals, visit the following natural areas:

## ARIZONA
Canyon de Chelly National Monument
Casa Grande Ruins National Monument
Chiricahua National Monument
Coronado National Memorial
Grand Canyon National Park
Montezuma Castle National Monument
Navajo National Monument
Organ Pipe Cactus National Monument
Saguaro National Park
Tonto National Monument
Walnut Canyon National Monument
Wupatki/Sunset Crater Volcano National Monument

## NEVADA
Lake Mead National Recreation Area

## NEW MEXICO
Bandelier National Monument
Capulin Volcano National Monument
Carlsbad Caverns National Park
Chaco Culture National Historical Park
El Malpais National Monument
Gila Cliff Dwellings National Monument
White Sands National Monument

## TEXAS
Big Bend National Park
Big Thicket National Preserve
Lake Meredith National Recreation Area

In addition, the Southwest is home to many other national parks, national wildlife refuges, national forests, state and county parks, and private preserves, which are all excellent places to find reptiles and amphibians. Most visitor centers compile species lists that tell you which animals live in that preserve.

Randall D. Babb

## WATCH BUT DON'T HANDLE

Because a number of snakes and one lizard in the Southwest are venomous—and potentially dangerous—it is important that you do not pick up or closely approach snakes or Gila monsters, our venomous lizard. When hiking, watch where you sit or put your feet and hands at all times of the year, since a few warm days can entice any reptile out from its winter home. By including venomous reptiles in this book, the authors are not endorsing handling or approaching potentially dangerous animals. Always enjoy snakes and Gila monsters from a distance.

## ABOUT THIS BOOK

Although the title says *common* reptiles and amphibians, we've sneaked in a few that are less than common, but interesting because of their ecology and habits or perhaps even because of their rarity. These include the elusive vine snake, coral snake, and Gila monster, which is our only venomous lizard and is uncommonly seen though not rare.

We define the Southwest as southeastern California, Arizona, New Mexico, west Texas, southwestern Oklahoma, southern Colorado, Utah, and Nevada.

To successfully identify a species using this book, pay close attention not only to the photograph and physical description of the animal, but to its habitat and range information as well. For example, if you are visiting a park in the desert, you would expect to see a desert spiny lizard rather than a Clark's spiny lizard because the latter usually live in oak woodlands. Or if you see a large land turtle in eastern New Mexico it's probably a box turtle rather than a desert tortoise, since desert tortoises live only in the far southwestern part of the state.

We also mention particular habits that make identification easier, such as the peculiar foraging gait of whiptail lizards or the favorite basking sites of chuckwallas. Behavior is often a very important element of species identification, so don't forget to observe what an animal is doing as well as what it looks like.

Regarding size, the information in this book is for total length, nose-to-tail—of each animal. The size range listed is from smallest to largest adult animal on record; most individuals of the species will fall somewhere in the middle. Colors are a bit more arbitrary than size, so take them as a guideline only. Age, habitat, and lighting can affect the color of any individual reptile or amphibian.

The primary name chosen for each animal is its most commonly used title in the Southwest, but others do exist. Whenever possible we have listed alternative common names for each species, as well as Spanish names.

# SNAKES

WESTERN DIAMONDBACK RATTLESNAKE

Randall D. Babb

SNAKES ARE IMPORTANT AND ABUNDANT MEMBERS OF SOUTHWESTERN ecosystems. They eat rodents, birds, eggs, frogs, toads, lizards, insects, and other snakes, all of which they swallow whole—their jaws expand greatly to accommodate meals much larger than their heads. These scaled reptiles live in the Southwest from low deserts to high mountain tops—some more than 9,000 feet. Although legless, they get around efficiently and quickly by contracting powerful muscles in alternating waves; many can even climb trees.

Snakes survey their surroundings in unique ways. Their constantly flicking tongues sample particles in the air, which a special organ in their palates "smells." Most snakes have good eyesight, but they do not have external ear openings. Instead, they detect ground vibrations through specialized bones in their skulls. Often they will feel your presence rather than see you—don't try to sneak up on a snake.

Some snakes lay eggs while others give birth to tiny, live young. All snakes periodically shed their skins as they continue to grow throughout their lives, which in the wild could last as long as twenty years or more.

Snakes are *ectotherms*—they cannot regulate their body temperature internally and must gain their heat in the environment. Look for them sunning on roads, trails, or rocks during the warm months, March through November. During the hottest months, they will be more active at dawn and dusk. In winter, most snakes hibernate and you are not likely to see them out; however, keep in mind that a succession of warm days may be enough to bring some snakes out of their winter torpor.

# 1 · Western Diamondback Rattlesnake
## *Crotalus atrox*

Western diamondbacks can reach legendary size—more than six feet long. Three photographs pinned to a bulletin board in a desert cafe attest to the diet of such hefty rattlers: a cottontail rabbit, swallowed whole—going-going-gone.

The second-largest rattlesnake species in the United States (only the eastern diamondback is bigger), western diamondbacks average about three feet long, with five being a normal maximum. Rattlesnakes are members of the pit viper family, so-called because they have a pair of pits between their eyes and nostrils. The pits are heat receptors that allow the snake to strike accurately at warm-bodied prey, even in complete darkness. Mice and kangaroo rats, two dietary staples of diamondbacks, often succumb within minutes to the venom. The snake then tracks down the carcass by scent.

The western diamondback is brownish to grayish overall, with a row of dark diamonds with light borders running down its back.

The last few inches of the tail sport a series of evenly spaced white and black rings, giving rise to the old nickname "coontail."

| | |
|---|---|
| **SIZE** | 30 to 84 in. (76 to 213 cm) |
| **HABITAT** | Low deserts to coniferous forests, but prefers arid and semiarid deserts, especially brushy areas and rocky outcrops from plains to foothills; sea level to about 7,000 f. |
| **RANGE** | Throughout most of central and southern New Mexico and Arizona (excluding the Mogollon Plateau); also southeastern California, Arkansas, Texas, Oklahoma; south into Mexico to northern Sinaloa and San Luis Potosi, as well as Baja California |
| **ALSO KNOWN AS** | coontail; *vibora, cascabel* (Spanish) |

# 2 · Rock Rattlesnake
## *Crotalus lepidus*

| | |
|---|---|
| **SIZE** | 15 to 33 in. (38 to 83 cm) |
| **HABITAT** | Talus-covered slopes, rocky hillsides, streambeds, and canyons; from 2,000 ft. to over 9,000 ft. |
| **RANGE** | Southeastern Arizona, southwestern and southern New Mexico, southwestern Texas; south through the Sierra Madre into central Mexico |
| **ALSO KNOWN AS** | Banded, mottled, or green rock rattlesnake |

As its name suggests, this rattlesnake frequents rocky areas. If encountered in the open, rock rattlesnakes will often lie quietly, relying on camouflage to avoid detection. Hikers who dislodge rocks on steep slopes might hear a startled rock rattlesnake rattling from a nearby crevice.

The rock rattlesnake is a beautiful mottled gray, pinkish, or even mint green, with a series of narrow, jagged-edged or zigzag dark bands crossing the back. It is a small rattlesnake, rarely exceeding thirty inches in length.

Lizards are the preferred meal for rock rattlesnakes, although they will dine on small mammals, frogs, and other snakes. The tails of juvenile rock rattlesnakes are yellow. According to several witnesses, the snakes wiggle their bright tails to lure in curious lizards for an easy meal. Adults, which lose their yellow tail color, apparently do not exhibit this behavior, known as "caudal luring."

The rock rattlesnake's hollow fangs, like those of other rattlesnakes, are imbedded in a bone that rotates, allowing the fangs to fold back along the jaw when the snake's mouth is closed. Rattlesnakes shed their fangs periodically; new ones continuously develop behind the existing fangs and immediately replace shed ones.

Throughout the winter, rock rattlesnakes hibernate deep in crevices where the temperature—of both rocks and snakes—stays slightly above freezing.

Randall D. Babb

# 8 · Black-tailed Rattlesnake
## *Crotalus molossus*

Randall D. Babb

Perhaps the most beautiful of all rattlesnakes, black-tails sport a similar scale pattern to the diamondback, but the colors are sharply contrasting olive greens, yellows, browns, and blacks. This brilliant pattern plus the all-black tail make identification easy (although a few black-tails have black-banded tails, rather than all-black).

Black-tailed rattlesnakes are especially common in rocky canyons and along ridgelines. In Mexico they live near sea level, but in the U.S. they more often inhabit higher elevations, in oak or pine woodlands. Black-tailed rattlesnakes are most active after the sun's warmth reaches deep into the cracks and crevices where they hibernate—or *brumate*, as herpetologists sometimes describe the torpor into which a reptile sinks when cold.

Tracking studies using surgically implanted radio transmitters indicate that paired black-tailed rattlesnakes sometimes stay together for several weeks after mating. It's possible the male stays with the female to prevent other males from attempting to mate with her.

| | |
|---|---|
| **SIZE** | 28 to 48 in. (70 to 122 cm) |
| **HABITAT** | Rocky canyons, steep slopes, and ridgelines, from mesquite grasslands to pine-oak woodlands; from sea level to 9,600 ft., but mostly above 3,500 ft. |
| **RANGE** | Central and southern Arizona; central and southern New Mexico; southwestern and central Texas; south to central Mexico |
| **ALSO KNOWN AS** | Black-tail, blacktail; *cascabel cola negra* (Spanish) |

# 4 · Mojave Rattlesnake
## *Crotalus scutulatus*

| | |
|---|---|
| **SIZE** | 24 to 51 in. (60 to 129 cm) |
| **HABITAT** | Foothills from near sea level to about 6,000 ft. |
| **RANGE** | From central California into southwestern Nevada and far southwestern Utah; northwestern, central, and southern Arizona; extreme southwestern and extreme southern New Mexico; southwestern Texas; south to central Mexico |
| **ALSO KNOWN AS** | Mohave rattlesnake, green Mojave rattlesnake |

The Mojave rattlesnake is easily confused with the western diamondback. One positive difference is not recommended for field observation: Mojaves have just a couple of large scales between their eyes on top of the head, while diamondbacks have many smaller scales. You need to be dangerously close to make that distinction. Another Mojave rattlesnake trait is also useless for field identification—this species produces the most potent venom of any rattlesnake.

In keeping with its armament, the Mojave's attitude is belligerent: it coils and rattles aggressively at any intrusion. However, like all snakes its chief aim is to escape unmolested, and if left alone when discovered will quickly disappear. Mojaves are active from spring through fall, when they hunt mostly rodents.

Like other rattlesnakes, the Mojave rattlesnake gains an additional rattle segment each time it sheds its skin. Since the frequency of shedding is variable, it is impossible to determine the age of a rattlesnake by counting the number of segments as years, despite persistent folklore. Also, sections often break off, leaving an incomplete rattle. It has even been reported that rodents sometimes gnaw off a segment or two while the snake is hibernating. That's a daring way to grab a snack.

# 5 · Tiger Rattlesnake
## *Crotalus tigris*

| | |
|---|---|
| **SIZE** | 18 to 36 in. (45 to 90 cm) |
| **HABITAT** | Hillsides and canyons in deserts and desert grassland; sea level to about 4,800 ft. |
| **RANGE** | South-central Arizona; south through Sonora, Mexico to the Gulf of California coast |

This dramatically named rattlesnake is so called not because of any particularly fierce disposition, but because of the tigerlike crossbands along its back. The tiger has a somewhat chunky appearance, which is emphasized by its relatively tiny head. This and its three-foot maximum length apparently restrict its diet to small rodents such as pocket mice and deer mice, as well as lizards. The tiger's venom, however, is very potent, displaying some of the same neurotoxic (affecting the central nervous system) qualities as the Mojave rattlesnake.

Desert hillsides and canyons, particularly where saguaros, ocotillos, and palo verde trees grow, are preferred habitats for the tiger rattlesnake. It is a largely nocturnal species, active from spring through fall. The tiger's hunting pattern seems to alternate between waiting quietly in coiled ambush and actively searching for prey.

Compared to other rattlesnakes, little is known of the tiger rattlesnake's reproduction pattern. Mating probably occurs in spring. Like other rattlesnakes, the young are live-born rather than hatched from eggs.

Randall D. Babb

# 6 · Sidewinder Rattlesnake
## *Crotalus cerastes*

C. Allan Morgan

The sidewinder has evolved a unique method of locomotion. It lifts most of its body off the ground and throws a loop forward, leaving a strange series of separated, J-shaped tracks. This "sidewinding" gait provides more traction for moving quickly across the soft sand in its preferred habitat. Because less of the snake's belly touches the hot sand, sidewinding might also keep the snake's body temperature from reaching dangerous levels. Contrary to some belief, though, sidewinders don't always use the sidewinding gait. They also slither like other snakes.

Even when not sidewinding, the sidewinder is easy to identify by the little horn-like projections above each eye. The purpose of these is not clear—theories include everything from sunshades to protection from underground obstacles. Sidewinders are largely nocturnal, waiting out hot days in rodent burrows, or coiling beneath the shade of a bush. To further insulate themselves from the heat, they shift their bodies from side to side until they are almost buried, with only the edges of the coils showing. This trick is called "cratering." Look for tell-tale saucer-shaped depressions under bushes.

Like all rattlesnakes, sidewinders bear live young. The average number is eight to ten, although up to eighteen have been recorded. The young are only about eight inches long at birth in late summer, but like all juvenile rattlesnakes they already have fully developed fangs (and venom) and a single, tiny prerattle button. They start out completely on their own and instinctively begin to hunt prey such as juvenile lizards.

| | |
|---|---|
| **SIZE** | 17 to 33 in. (42 to 82 cm) |
| **HABITAT** | Sandy flats in creosote and mesquite deserts, occasionally rocky slopes; from below sea level to about 6,000 ft. |
| **RANGE** | Southwestern California; southern Nevada and extreme southwestern Utah; western and west-central Arizona |
| **ALSO KNOWN AS** | horned rattlesnake; *vibora de cuernitos* (Spanish) |

# 7 · Western Blind Snake
## *Leptotyphlops humilis*

Randall D. Babb

This snake might be tiny—rarely longer than ten inches—but it shrugs off attacks by ants to feed on eggs and larvae within the ant colony. Imagine having to fight ten thousand angry dachshunds to get to your refrigerator! The blind snake locates these colonies by following the pheromone trail left by the insects. Termites are another favorite meal; other arthropods such as small millipedes or centipedes round off the diet. Blind snakes, in turn, are one of the major dietary staples of coral snakes.

At first glance, blind snakes resemble worms more than snakes. Their vestigial eyes are tiny black dots, and the head is nothing more than a blunt end on the body. Look closely, though, and you'll see the sheen of very smooth, hexagonal-shaped scales.

Although they spend much of their lives underground, blind snakes roam the surface at night or around dusk during the summer months. In a flashlight beam they shine noticeably.

| | |
|---|---|
| **SIZE** | 7 to 16 in. (18 to 41 cm) |
| **HABITAT** | Loose soil, canyon bottoms, patches of soil on rocky hills, and in urban areas; below sea level in low desert sinks to around 5,000 ft. |
| **RANGE** | West-central and southern Arizona and extreme southwestern New Mexico; also extreme southern Nevada, southwestern Utah; south to Colima and Baja California, Mexico |
| **ALSO KNOWN AS** | Worm snake |

# 8 · Rosy Boa
## *Lichanura trivirgata*

| | |
|---|---|
| **SIZE** | 24 to 44 in. (60 to 110 cm) |
| **HABITAT** | Deserts, often near oases or temporary water sources; from sea level to about 4,500 ft. |
| **RANGE** | Southwestern Arizona; southern California; Baja California and western Sonora, Mexico |
| **ALSO KNOWN AS** | *corcúa roja* (Spanish) |

Although it is related to twenty-foot-long pythons and anacondas, the rosy boa seldom exceeds three feet. It does use the same constricting method to capture prey, first grabbing the animal with a bite, then wrapping powerful coils around it until the intended meal suffocates or its heart stops. Although pythons have been known to eat goats and small antelope, rosy boas stick to mice, kangaroo rats, and birds.

Rosy boas are beautiful snakes: beige or yellowish to true rose overall, with sometimes indistinct darker stripes running the length of the body, and a creamy belly. Like most boas, the rosy boa has vestigial hind limbs, visible as tiny spurs near the cloacal opening, or vent, of males. These are the only visible remnants of the snake's four-legged ancestry.

Rosy boas live in the low, rocky deserts and shrublands of western Arizona. They are fairly slow-moving snakes; look for them as they cross roads. Unfortunately, automobiles cause significant mortality to rosy boa populations near highways. The rosy boa is popular as a pet because of its gentle nature; this popularity could also prove a threat to wild populations if collecting escalates out of control.

Randall D. Babb

# 9 · Black-necked Garter Snake
## *Thamnophis cyrtopsis*

C. Allan Morgan

Robert & Linda Mitchell

A snake swimming through water is a startling sight, but that's where you're likely to find black-necked garter snakes. They are common in Arizona and New Mexico along streams and rivers, in ponds and lakes, and even in cattle watering tanks. They zip through the water hunting tadpoles and adult frogs and toads, along with fish and crustaceans, and the occasional lizard and earthworm.

Garter snakes rarely bite when handled, but they have an even more effective deterrent: they release a foul-smelling musk from their vent. After contact with this pungent cocktail, most predators steer clear of garter snakes.

In the spring, adult black-necked garter snakes often bask on riverbanks or pond edges before they hunt. You can identify a black-necked garter snake by the black spots on each side of the back of the head and a pale side stripe that is two scales wide. In summer, females may give birth to up to twenty young. The little five-inch garter snakes immediately begin to fend for themselves.

| | |
|---|---|
| **SIZE** | 16 to 43 in. (40 to 107 cm) |
| **HABITAT** | In or near water; from sea level to about 8,700 ft. |
| **RANGE** | Central and eastern Arizona; widespread in New Mexico except far east; southwestern Utah; southern Colorado; southwestern Texas; widespread in Mexico |
| **ALSO KNOWN AS** | blackneck garter snake; *culebra de agua* (Spanish) |

# *10* · Western Hognose Snake
## *Heterodon nasicus*

| | |
|---|---|
| **SIZE** | 16 to 36 in. (40 to 90 cm) |
| **HABITAT** | Sandy or loose soils suitable for burrowing, especially in grasslands and open woodlands; from near sea level to about 8,000 ft. |
| **RANGE** | Northeastern, central, and southern New Mexico; southeastern Arizona; north through the plains states into southern Canada; south into northeastern Mexico |
| **ALSO KNOWN AS** | Spreading adder, spreadheaded viper; *trompa de cochi* (Spanish) |

Hognose snakes are famous for their habit of "playing possum" when threatened. When first approached, the hognose often hisses and strikes pugnaciously, although it rarely bites. If this bravado fails, the snake takes a different tack: it rolls onto its back, writhing as if in death throes, and then lies still with mouth open and tongue hanging out. If the observer turns the snake upright, it will immediately flip back upside-down as if to convince the skeptic that it really is dead.

Thick-bodied snakes with virtually no neck, hognose snakes have an unmistakable upturned and protruding scale on the snout. They use this scale, or *rostral*, for digging up prey, which can include toads, lizards, small snakes, and reptile eggs. Enlarged teeth at the back of the jaw help the hognose hold onto its prey, but they might also introduce the mildly venomous saliva. This could be viewed as an early evolutionary step to a more sophisticated venom apparatus, like that of the rattlesnakes.

Randall D. Babb

# 11 · Sonoran Whipsnake
## *Masticophis bilineatus*

Randall D. Babb

Sonoran whipsnakes are slender and fast-moving—like a whip. An observer often gets only a moment for identification before the snake disappears into the undergrowth, or into a bush or tree, since they are excellent climbers. Sonoran whipsnakes usually live in canyons or near streambeds, especially where vegetation is dense. They have large eyes and grayish, blue-gray, or faded olive bodies, with lighter stripes on each side that fade toward the tail.

Whipsnakes are often active throughout the day, hunting on the ground and in trees for frogs, lizards, and birds. They are not venomous, nor do they constrict their prey—they simply grab and swallow it whole.

Watching any snake swallow something bigger than its head is amazing. Not only can the snake expand its jaw to prodigious size, it is able to breathe throughout the process. Its trachea is modified into a snorkel-like tube that extends out the bottom of the mouth. The trachea and its opening, the glottis, are ringed with cartilage to prevent their collapsing while the unfortunate mouse or bird makes its last journey.

A similar species to the Sonoran whipsnake, the striped whipsnake (*M. taeniatus*), lives in northern Arizona and across most of New Mexico.

| | |
|---|---|
| **SIZE** | 24 to 67 in. (60 to 170 cm) |
| **HABITAT** | From deserts to mountain forests, especially in canyons or drainages and in dense vegetation; from near sea level to about 6,000 ft. |
| **RANGE** | Central and southwestern Arizona; far southeastern New Mexico; south through western Mexico |

# 12 · Coachwhip
## *Masticophis flagellum*

Cecil R. Schwalbe

Herpetologists jokingly change this snake's genus to *Nasty-cophis*, in tribute to its belligerent nature when cornered by a would-be human captor. It repeatedly strikes and bites, sometimes even advancing on the threat, inflicting non-life-threatening but annoying lacerations to the hands and arms of the victim. Early Spanish explorers created the myth of the coachwhip's ability to stand on its head and use its long tail to flog anyone unlucky enough to cross its path.

If an escape route is left open, however, the coachwhip can disappear with amazing speed. Coachwhips are frequently spotted crossing roads—even on hot summer days (they are one of the few diurnal desert snakes )—but they are rarely seen again by anyone who stops to search. Statistically, their top speed is only about four miles per hour.

Coachwhips can range to well over seven feet in length and are highly variable in color. They can be almost pure black, or nearly scarlet, or even a brownish color. Prey includes lizards, snakes, small mammals, birds, and frogs; also eggs, grasshoppers, and cicadas. Female coachwhips lay a clutch of about ten eggs in summer; hatchlings can be nearly fifteen inches long.

| | |
|---|---|
| **SIZE** | 36 to 102 in. (90 to 255 cm) |
| **HABITAT** | Varied, including deserts, desert grasslands, and pine-oak woodlands; from below sea level to about 7,700 ft. |
| **RANGE** | Widespread across the southwestern U.S. and Mexico; not found in northeastern Arizona or northwestern New Mexico |
| **ALSO KNOWN AS** | red racer or black racer, depending on color; *alicante* (Spanish) |

# 13 · Western Patch-nosed Snake
## *Salvadora hexalepis*

| | |
|---|---|
| **SIZE** | 20 to 46 in. (55 to 115 cm) |
| **HABITAT** | Deserts with either sandy or gravelly soils and open cover; from below sea level in low-desert sinks to about 7,000 ft. |
| **RANGE** | Northwestern, central, and southern Arizona; southern Utah, central and southern Nevada, and southern California; Baja California, Mexico |

The nose scale, or *rostral*, of the patch-nosed snake is enlarged and folded back like a triangular shield. Some researchers believe this assists them in digging up reptile eggs, which form part of their diet. When female patch-noses lay eggs, they also deposit a pheromone, which somehow prevents other patch-nosed snakes from eating the eggs.

Patch-nosed snakes are slender, a dark green-gray with a pale yellowish stripe down the center of the back and on the lower sides. They are fast-moving snakes, and sometimes even climb trees in search of prey such as lizards.

Patch-nosed snakes typically live in deserts, although they range from creosote-covered flatlands all the way up to oak woodlands. They seem to have a tolerance for wide temperature ranges and, depending on local climates, are active from March through November.

Randall D. Babb

Jonathan Hanson

# 14 · Green Rat Snake
## *Senticolis triaspis*

Randall D. Babb

Green rat snakes practice classic startle defense behavior. When disturbed, a green rat snake will suddenly open its mouth wide, revealing a bright white interior that is startling and threatening. In the case of the green rat snake, however, the "bark" is worse than the bite—they rarely bite or even hiss.

This beautiful snake is uniformly light green above, slightly paler below, with a slender head. It is a tropical species, found in Central America and up through Mexico, barely reaching Arizona and far southwestern New Mexico. In our area green rat snakes typically live in mountains, especially along drainages or in canyons. Hikers sometimes see them crossing trails or forest roads, before these fast snakes disappear into the brush.

Little is known about the reproductive or food habits of the green rat snake. A couple of dissected specimens had mice in their digestive tracts. Some researchers report that green rat snakes also eat lizards and birds. It was long believed, because of their green color, that these snakes were primarily tree-dwellers. However, green rat snakes are seen on the ground more often than in trees, so their reputed arboreal preferences have been discounted.

| | |
|---|---|
| **SIZE** | 24 to 50 in. (60 to 125 cm) |
| **HABITAT** | Riparian corridors with sycamore, walnut, and oak trees, as well as oak woodlands; 2,500 ft. to about 7,000 ft. |
| **RANGE** | Extreme southwestern New Mexico; southeastern Arizona to the Baboquivari Mts.; south through the Sierra Madre in Mexico to Central America |

# *15* · Regal Ringneck Snake
## *Diadophis punctatus*

Cecil R. Schwalbe

Although not semi-aquatic like garter snakes, ringneck snakes do prefer moist habitats, either near water or where the water table is close to the surface. They live across much of the U.S. and Mexico. In the Southwest they are common except in the dry western deserts.

Ringneck snakes are very smooth-scaled, with a rich olive to blue-gray above, a brilliant red or orange belly, and a neck ring of a similar color. When alarmed, the snake will hide its head and coil its tail into a tight disk, flashing its bright underside to startle or distract possible predators. If further harassed, it will exude musk, an even more effective deterrent.

As you would guess from its habitat, the ringneck snake preys on other animals associated with water. Salamanders, frogs, worms, and slugs are mainstays of a notably slimy diet, although it will also eat lizards and small snakes. The ringneck shows evidence of a primitive venom apparatus: enlarged (but not hollow or even grooved) rear teeth, and saliva that may have a paralytic effect on small prey.

Snakes like the ringneck are fascinating studies in evolution, since one can imagine the slow progression to more potent venom to kill prey more quickly, and longer, more sophisticated fangs to deliver it more efficiently.

| | |
|---|---|
| **SIZE** | 8 to 30 in. (20 to 75 cm) |
| **HABITAT** | Moist habitats in woodlands, forests, and grasslands; from sea level to about 7,000 ft. |
| **RANGE** | Widespread across eastern and central U.S., all of New Mexico except the northwest; central and southeastern Arizona; populations in Utah, Nevada, and Pacific Coast states; south to central Mexico |

# 16 · Gopher Snake
## *Pituophis melanoleucus*

| | |
|---|---|
| **SIZE** | 36 to 110 in. (90 to 260 cm) |
| **HABITAT** | Deserts, desert grasslands, cultivated fields, oak and pine-oak woodlands, pine and fir forests; from sea level to about 9,000 ft. |
| **RANGE** | Widespread across the U.S.; into southwestern Canada; south through Mexico into Guatemala |

Gopher snakes are great actors. Not only do they look a little like rattlesnakes at first glance, when harassed a gopher snake will coil up, flatten its head, hiss and strike, and even vibrate its tail. While this might work to drive off possible predators, unfortunately it also gets many gopher snakes killed by frightened humans who mistake them for the real thing.

Like rattlesnakes, gopher snakes are extremely effective controllers of rodents, which constitute the majority of their diet, augmented by birds and eggs. They kill by constriction, or, in a confined burrow, by pressing the animal against the tunnel wall with a single loop of the body.

The gopher snake is one of the most common and widespread snakes in the United States, with nearly a dozen recognized subspecies. In the Southwest it lives from sea level, in low-desert sinks, up into pine-fir forests at 9,000 feet. Also called the bull snake, the gopher is the longest snake in either Arizona or New Mexico, sometimes exceeding eight feet, although six feet is a more common length.

Gopher snakes are active throughout the day in spring and fall; in summer they become more nocturnal. In late spring the female lays up to nineteen eggs, which hatch in late summer. If food is plentiful, she will sometimes lay a second clutch of eggs within a few weeks of the first. This strategy is one of the reasons the gopher snake is so plentiful and successful across North America.

Robert & Linda Mitchell

# 17 · Long-nosed Snake
## *Rhinocheilus lecontei*

| | |
|---|---|
| **SIZE** | 20 to 41 in. (50 to 104 cm) |
| **HABITAT** | Plains, valleys and low hills in deserts and desert grasslands; sea level to about 5,500 ft. |
| **RANGE** | Northeastern, central, and southern New Mexico; southern, west-central, and northwestern Arizona; parts of California, Nevada, and Utah; also Texas and Oklahoma; south through Mexico |

The pointed nose and countersunk lower jaw of the long-nosed snake hint at its proficiency as a burrower in loose soil. Like all other snakes, instead of eyelids the long-nosed snake has clear scales covering its eyes, which protect them against abrasion. These scales are shed and renewed with the skin, so they function like the peel-off films on the face shields of open-cockpit race car drivers—if one gets scratched or marred, a fresh one can soon take its place.

Long-nosed snakes hunt lizards and mice in the desert valleys and plains of the Southwest below 6,000 feet elevation. In spite of this apparent preference for a warm climate, they have been seen hunting at temperatures as low as sixty degrees Fahrenheit—virtual Arctic conditions for a snake. They are often crepuscular—active at dawn and dusk—or nocturnal. Sharp-eyed drivers can spot them crossing roads at night.

Long-nosed snakes lay fairly small clutches of from three to nine eggs, but evidence suggests some individuals might lay two clutches during warm years, if food is plentiful.

Randall D. Babb

# 18 · Common Kingsnake
## *Lampropeltis getula*

Randall D. Babb

Legend has it that kingsnakes' arch enemies are rattlesnakes, which they pursue and fight in deadly battles. Furthermore, legend holds that kingsnakes are immune to rattler venom. In this case, legend is half correct—kingsnakes are immune to the venom, although many other snakes also display such a resistance. Contrary to folklore, though, kingsnakes don't single out rattlesnakes to persecute.

What kingsnakes do spend a lot of time pursuing are mice, lizards, and birds. Kingsnakes also eat other snakes—occasionally ones longer than themselves, and sometimes rattlesnakes, hence the legendary "battles."

Common kingsnakes are usually pale yellow or white with wide bands of black or dark brown; sometimes they appear mostly black with narrow yellow bands. A subspecies, the desert kingsnake *(L.g. splendida)*, sometimes lacks bands altogether and is merely speckled with yellow.

A related species, the Sonoran mountain kingsnake (*Lampropeltis pyromelana*), sports a brightly colored, banded pattern similar to the coral snake. It's beautiful, but too often gets mountain kingsnakes confused with "deadly" coral snakes. The easiest differentiation is in the order of the colored bands: "Red on yellow, kill a fellow; red on black, venom lack." A bit sensational, but easy to remember.

| | |
|---|---|
| **SIZE** | 30 to 82 in. (75 to 208 cm) |
| **HABITAT** | Deserts, riparian areas, woodlands, and forests; sea level to about 7,000 ft. |
| **RANGE** | Across the southern half of the U.S.; all of Arizona except northeastern and east-central; southern and east-central New Mexico; south through Mexico |
| **ALSO KNOWN AS** | desert kingsnake; *coralillo falsa* (Spanish), for mountain kingsnake |

# 19 · Western Shovel-nosed Snake
## *Chionactis occipitalis*

| | |
|---|---|
| **SIZE** | 10 to 17 in. (25 to 42 cm) |
| **HABITAT** | Deserts with loose, sandy soil, or rocky hillsides with sandy patches; sea level to about 4,700 ft. |
| **RANGE** | Western Arizona; southern Nevada; southeastern California |

Shovel-nosed snakes are efficient at moving underground, but the technique they use is closer to swimming than burrowing. Their preferred habitat is loose desert sand, in which they wriggle back and forth, moving like fish through water and leaving no tunnel behind. Tiny valves in the snake's nostrils prevent sand from getting in, and the recessed mouth and smooth scales further the "streamlined" design.

The shovel-nose lives in the hottest and driest deserts of western Arizona. It stays buried through the day, where the temperature a foot down can be 50 degrees cooler than at the surface. It emerges during the night to hunt for insects, spiders, and scorpions. If alarmed, a shovel-nosed snake quickly dives into the sand.

The diminutive shovel-nosed snake is another species that observers confuse with the coral snake, an impression strengthened by the similar size of the two. But the shovel-nose's red markings, if not absent altogether, are clearly saddles, not bands as in the coral snake; also the coral snake has a black head instead of yellow.

Randall D. Babb

# 20 · Vine Snake
## *Oxybelis aeneus*

Randall D. Babb

L ook closely at that clump of wild grape vines: is that a twig or a snake? If you're a lizard, you'd better be right if you think it's a twig. Vine snakes are specialized arboreal snakes that eat lizards.

Shaped and colored exactly as its alternate name suggests, the brown vine snake is extremely difficult to spot. But at night you can sometimes pick one out by flashlight, napping in a loose coil on top of low shrubs.

Vine snakes have primitive, grooved fangs in the rear of their mouths, and venom just potent enough to subdue the lizards that make up virtually their entire menu. A researcher who was bitten in the hand reported numbness for about 12 hours.

In Arizona, vine snakes live in brushy hillsides and canyon bottoms in just a few mountain ranges along the Mexican border.

Randall D. Babb

| | |
|---|---|
| **SIZE** | 36 to 60 in. (90 to 152 cm) |
| **HABITAT** | Riparian corridors and adjacent brushy hillsides; sea level to about 5,200 ft. |
| **RANGE** | Extreme south-central Arizona; south through western Mexico and Central America to Brazil |
| **ALSO KNOWN AS** | Brown vine snake, tropical vine snake; *huirotillo, bejuquillo* (Spanish) |

# 21 · Lyre Snake
## *Trimorphodon biscutatus*

C. Allan Morgan

Lyre snakes are nighttime specialists. Their pupils are elliptical like those of cats, so they can see better in darkness. Moving along rocky ground or slipping up a steep rock face, they hunt in crevices and caves for one of their favorite types of prey: bats.

Rock-dwelling lizards, mice, and birds are also part of lyre snakes' diet. They subdue their prey with both constriction and weak venom injected through grooved rear teeth. Although these teeth are enlarged, the snake apparently has to chew a lot to fully introduce the venom. Even then, it seems to be more effective on lizards than on mammals.

Named for the lyre- or V-shaped marking on the top of the head, lyre snakes may not conform to the typical spring egg-laying, summer hatching breeding cycle of most other southwestern snakes. If captive specimens are any indicator, they might lay eggs any time from December through September.

| | |
|---|---|
| **SIZE** | 18 to 45 in. (45 to 112 cm) |
| **HABITAT** | Rocky areas in canyons, hills, and human-made structures; sea level to about 7,400 ft. |
| **RANGE** | Northwestern and southern Arizona; southwestern New Mexico; southern California and Nevada; southwestern Texas; south through Baja California and Sonora, Mexico |

# 22 · Night Snake
### *Hypsiglena torquata*

| | |
|---|---|
| **SIZE** | 12 to 26 in. (90 to 152 cm) |
| **HABITAT** | Deserts to pine forests; sea level to about 8,700 ft. |
| **RANGE** | Widespread throughout the Southwest, including all of Arizona and New Mexico, except far north-central; south through Baja California, and mainland Mexico |
| **ALSO KNOWN AS** | Fanged night snake; *culebra, víbora muda* (Spanish) |

The night snake has vertical pupils and the same brownish coloration as the lyre snake, but instead of a V-shaped mark on the top of the head, the night snake has large dark blotches right where its ears would be—if snakes had ears.

Suiting both its name and cat-like pupils, the night snake is almost exclusively a nocturnal hunter. With its short rear fangs and mild venom it paralyzes lizards and small snakes, and sometimes frogs and toads. In captivity some have eaten other night snakes, but it is not known if they do so in the wild.

Night snakes rarely bite defensively, but when touched they often writhe violently. It's possible this reaction could startle an inquisitive predator long enough for the snake to make its escape. Other night snakes have been reported to coil into a tight ball with the head in the center when threatened. This behavior must be an effective deterrent to predators, even though it seems to do nothing more than create a bite-sized package.

Randall D. Babb

# 23 · Western Coral Snake
## *Micruroides euryxanthus*

| | |
|---|---|
| **SIZE** | 12 to 20 in. (30 to 50 cm) |
| **HABITAT** | Deserts and desert grasslands, as well as riparian corridors; sea level to about 5,800 ft. |
| **RANGE** | Southern Arizona; far southwestern New Mexico; south through Sonora, Mexico |
| **ALSO KNOWN AS** | Arizona coral snake; *coralillo* (Spanish) |

The diminutive coral snake has an almost mythic reputation—it is, after all, related to cobras and mambas and produces an extremely toxic venom. Yet records show that not one human death has been reported from the bite of a western coral snake.

Coral snakes are not rare, but they are rarely seen and are unaggressive if harassed by a would-be predator. Also, an average western coral snake, all fourteen or so inches of it, would have a difficult time getting its tiny mouth around even the little finger of a human.

Unlike rattlesnakes, the coral snake's front-mounted fangs are fixed in place and fit into little pockets in the lower jaw. These fangs are so short (barely one thirty-second of an inch) that the snake often has trouble envenoming even its usual prey of blind snakes and small lizards; it simply grasps and swallows them.

When threatened, the coral snake has the interesting habit—in scientific terms—of "everting its cloaca" and making a distinct, repeated popping sound. We'll leave it to the reader to recall a more common expression for this habit.

Randall D. Babb

# LIZARDS

FROM THE DIMINUTIVE AND NOCTURNAL GECKOS TO THE LARGE and venomous Gila monster, lizards represent perhaps the most varied, fascinating, and abundant of all the reptiles. While most lizards have dry, scaly skin, four legs, and a long tail, some, such as the glass lizards, have no legs at all. And some are rounded and have short tails, such as horny "toads." Lizards also live in a variety of habitats, from arid deserts to wet coniferous forests, and from sand to trees to water environments.

Of all the reptiles, lizards are easiest to watch because they are abundant as well as most active during times when we can readily enjoy them. In the Southwest, lizards start to feed when the temperature rises—usually above sixty-five degrees Fahrenheit. During midday heat, they retreat into burrows and under rocks and debris piles. They emerge again in late afternoon. Most lizards hibernate through the winter, although a series of warm days might bring some out.

Lizard diets are hugely variable. Most of the smaller lizards are insectivores, some are herbivores, and others, such as the Gila monster and the spiny lizards, are carnivores and omnivores, respectively.

Most North American lizards lay eggs in moist earth, under leaf litter, or in decomposing wood; however, some do give birth to live young.

Larry Lindahl

MALE AND FEMALE COLLARED LIZARDS

# 24 · Gila Monster
## *Heloderma suspectum*

George H. H. Huey

Like the rattlesnake, the venomous Gila monster is has starred as chief villain in numerous movies and advertisements. But the fierce looks of this largest U.S. lizard are mostly just looks. Its slow gait is best suited for its preferred prey, which are baby mammals, especially rodents and rabbits, and eggs and nestling birds.

Gila monsters have bumpy bead-like scales with a geometric black-and-reddish (or sometimes pink or orange) pattern. Gila monsters are not rare, but since they spend a lot of time in underground dens, usually the same ones in a home range of about a square mile or less, few people see them. They are also wary, and perfectly camouflaged for the dappled shade where they hide from predators.

Contrary to popular belief, they are not nocturnal; you may find them lumbering across roads or trails on warm mornings or afternoons (and occasionally at night) in deserts, desert grasslands, or even up to oak or juniper woodlands. Like many reptiles they wait out extreme heat in cool burrows and gain most of their water needs from their prey. Their thick tails are fat reservoirs.

Bites from Gila monsters occur each year, usually when people attempt to handle them. Their venom, strictly a defensive agent, is highly toxic and can cause great pain and nausea.

| | |
|---|---|
| **SIZE** | 18 to 24 in. (45.7 to 61 cm) |
| **HABITAT** | Deserts, desert grasslands, up to edge of oak and juniper woodlands; from sea level to about 5,000 ft. |
| **RANGE** | From southwestern New Mexico west to Colorado River; north to extreme southwestern Utah; from just south of Mogollon Rim in Arizona south to Sinaloa, Mexico |
| **ALSO KNOWN AS** | *escorpión* (Spanish) |

# 25 · Western Banded Gecko
## *Coleonyx variegatus*

| | |
|---|---|
| **SIZE** | 4-1/2 to 6 in. (11.4 to 15 cm) |
| **HABITAT** | Deserts to oak woodlands and piñon-juniper woodlands, especially rocky areas but sometimes in sand dunes; sea level to 5,000 ft. |
| **RANGE** | Southeastern New Mexico west to coastal southern California, south through Baja; Sonora, Mexico, south to southern Sinaloa |
| **ALSO KNOWN AS** | *salamanquesa de franjas* (Spanish) |

This beautiful little lizard, with its pale pinkish and brown-banded translucent skin, seems far too delicate to live in the harsh deserts of the Southwest. But it thrives in deserts, grasslands, and even cities because it restricts its activity to nights, when humidity is up and heat down.

Western banded geckos frequent crevices, moist areas under rocks and debris, or rodent burrows where they hunt for insects and spiders. On warm nights, you might also see them on blacktop roads, their pale skin illuminated by your headlights. If you catch one, don't be surprised if it squeaks. The geckos you see on house or yard walls, especially around lights, are Mediterranean geckos, an introduced species that thrives in southwestern cities.

When geckos are threatened, they stand tall on their legs and hold their tails over their backs, similar to a scorpion; they even wiggle the tail. Some researchers think this mimicry might be an attempt to deter predators; others believe that the tail wiggling serves to divert a predator's attention, since geckos' tails, like those of many lizards, break off readily (and grow back) should they be grabbed.

George H. H. Huey

# 26 · Desert Iguana
## *Dipsosaurus dorsalis*

| | |
|---|---|
| **SIZE** | 10 to 16 in. (25.4 to 40.6 cm) |
| **HABITAT** | Deserts, especially with creosote, in valleys or bajadas; below sea level in low desert sinks to about 5,000 ft. |
| **RANGE** | Western Arizona; southern Nevada; southeastern California; south through Baja, and along the Gulf Coast of mainland Mexico |
| **ALSO KNOWN AS** | Desert crested lizard; *porohui* (Spanish) |

Mad dogs, Englishmen, and desert iguanas—the old saying could include—go out in the midday sun. Desert iguanas live in the hottest and driest parts of our North American deserts, in western Arizona, southern Nevada, and southeastern California. Their preferred habitats are the vast expanses of creosote scrub in low, flat desert valleys, where it seems little could survive. But desert iguanas are out and active on late summer mornings, when most other animals have retreated underground to wait out the heat.

Creosote provides more than habitat for the iguanas—they climb into the branches to feast on new leaves and fresh flower buds (and to get above the ground heat). They also dine on other plants and occasionally eat insects, carrion, and their own fecal pellets, an unsavory-sounding habit but an effective way to recycle the minute amount of moisture and nutrients that are otherwise lost.

The desert iguana has a pale, speckled pattern that matches the sandy soil where it lives. A row of enlarged, slightly protruding scales down the middle of its back distinguishes it from similar species. Females lay a clutch of three to eight eggs in late summer, burying them where they will stay warm but not too hot.

George H. H. Huey

# 27 · Common Collared Lizard
## *Crotaphytus collaris*

C. Allan Morgan

The collared lizard is a nimble inhabitant of rocky canyons and outcroppings, leaping from ledge to ledge and chasing down its prey—other lizards and insects—like a miniature *Tyrannosaurus*. In fact, at full speed the collared lizard often holds its front feet up and powers along using only the back legs, just like its extinct distant relative.

Collared lizards, especially the males, are highly territorial and will initiate belligerent displays, including rapid push-ups, at the approach of another lizard—or even a human. If the intruding lizard ignores this warning, the collared lizard will vigorously attack. If a human ignores the warning and attempts to capture the "pretty lizard doing push-ups," the collared lizard will vigorously bite.

The tails of collared lizards, unlike those of many other lizards, do not readily break off and regenerate if the animal is attacked. A squirming tail segment distracts a would be predator, often giving the tail's former owner a chance to escape. But collared lizards need their tails for balance while running and jumping, so the cost of such a decoy may be too great for this species, and they either lost the adaptation or it never evolved.

| | |
|---|---|
| **SIZE** | 8 to 14 in. (20 to 35.6 cm) |
| **HABITAT** | Rocky terrain in a variety of habitats, from deserts through pine-oak woodlands, especially with large boulders for sunning |
| **RANGE** | Most of Arizona and New Mexico; lower plains states; parts of Utah and Colorado; northern Mexico |
| **ALSO KNOWN AS** | mountain boomer; *lagartija de collar* (Spanish) |

# 28 · Long-nosed Leopard Lizard
## *Gambelia wislizenii*

Randall D. Babb

Fast and spotted just like its namesake, the leopard lizard further earns its name by biting fiercely if handled. Leopard lizards prey on other lizards and on many kinds of insects such as grasshoppers, crickets, and beetles, and they will also eat some plant material.

Unusual for lizards, or any reptile for that matter, leopard lizards can emit a shrill squeal if threatened. Their response to trouble can also change depending on the temperature. If it is warm, the lizard will try to escape; however, at lower temperatures its strategy might switch to a more aggressive resistance. This mercurial response makes sense, since a cold lizard can't run away as quickly as a warm one.

During the spring breeding season, a female leopard lizard develops reddish spots on her back and underside of her tail. These disappear by summer, after she lays up to eleven eggs.

| | |
|---|---|
| **SIZE** | 8 to 15 in. (22 to 38 cm) |
| **HABITAT** | Open deserts and desert grasslands; from sea level to about 6,000 ft. |
| **RANGE** | Throughout Arizona except for White Mountains; western and southern New Mexico; Utah and Nevada into Idaho and Oregon; southern California; south through Baja and northern mainland Mexico |

# $29$ · Common Chuckwalla
## *Sauromalus obesus*

| | |
|---|---|
| **SIZE** | 11 to 16-1/2 in. (27.9 to 41.9 cm) |
| **HABITAT** | Rock outcrops, lava flows, and rocky hillsides in deserts, especially with creosote bushes; from sea level to about 6,000 ft. |
| **RANGE** | Southern Nevada and Utah, south through western Arizona and along western and eastern coasts of the Gulf of California in Sonora and Baja; several subspecies live on some islands in the Gulf of California |
| **ALSO KNOWN AS** | chuckawalla; *iguana* (Spanish) |

Look closely at rocky outcrops in southwestern deserts—did that rock move? Well-camouflaged chuckwallas soak up late morning and afternoon sun on dark rocks, especially those of volcanic origin. They will  bask until their body temperatures reach 100 degrees before venturing out to feed.

These big lizards, which can grow up to almost seventeen inches long, are vegetarians. They need to eat a lot of plant material to support their large size—they will eat leaves, flowers, seeds, fruits, and grass. Juveniles sometimes eat insects, but adults are not known to continue the habit.

An adult chuckwalla has a black head, chest, and limbs and is reddish or gray over the rest of the body. Males have pale yellow tails, while the females and juveniles have dark-banded tails and sometimes bands on the body.

When fleeing predators such as hawks, coyotes, or humans, chuckwallas will crawl into rock crevices and then fill their lungs with air until they are wedged in tightly and safely.

Randall D. Babb

# 30 · Greater Earless Lizard
## *Cophosaurus texanus*

| | |
|---|---|
| **SIZE** | 3-1/4 to 7-1/4 in. (8 to 18.4 cm) |
| **HABITAT** | Sandy and sparsely vegetated areas in upland desert with cacti, mesquites, creosote, ocotillos, and palo verde trees; from 100 ft. to about 5,600 ft. |
| **RANGE** | Across the Southwest from west-central Arizona across New Mexico and into most of Texas; south into northeastern Mexico to Tamaulipas |

Now you see them, now you don't—greater earless lizards have a great disappearing act. When danger approaches, they dive under loose soil, debris, or sand and quickly burrow out of sight. Scales around their eyes, nostrils, and mouth prevent them from filling with dirt, and their ears have no external openings, although they can hear.

Greater earless lizards are medium-sized—about six inches long—and beautifully patterned. Depending on the color of the soil where they live, they can be ornately flecked gray, brown, orange, and reddish. Both sexes have two black crescents along the sides of their bellies near their hind legs, and black bars on the undersides of their tails. Males sport blue, greenish, and/or yellow on their sides. When ready to mate, females develop bright orange patches under their chins.

Greater earless lizards are keen insect hunters. They prefer upland desert sparsely covered with cacti and thorn shrubs—look for them darting across open, sandy areas such as dry washes as they search for grasshoppers, spiders, butterflies, moths, and other arthropods throughout the day.

During spring and summer mating season, both male and female greater earless lizards engage in solo territorial "dances" that might include head bobbing and leg lifting.

C. Allan Morgan

# 31 · Zebra-tailed Lizard
## Callisaurus draconoides

Zebra-tailed lizards have a unique approach to dealing with predators: instead of hiding, they wave their black-striped tails at them. Scientific opinion is split on why they offer this seemingly suicidal "here-I-am" signal. One thought is that the wave indicates to the predator—a roadrunner or coyote, for example—that the lizard has seen it and pursuit would be futile. Another theory is that the predator will pounce on the waving tail, which breaks off readily from the body and thus distracts the predator while the lizard escapes. Zebra-tailed lizards, like many lizards, can regrow their tails.

C. Allan Morgan

These slender, seven-inch-long lizards are fast runners. But they save their speed for escaping danger rather than for hunting. They are "sit-and-wait" predators, preferring to grab various insects that pass by, including cater-pillars, beetles, bees, grasshoppers, and spiders. Occasionally they will also eat other lizards.

Zebra-tailed lizards breed in spring and summer. Like their relatives the greater earless lizards, zebra-tails engage in territorial displays such as head bobbing and limb waving.

| | |
|---|---|
| **SIZE** | 6 to 9-1/8 in. (15.2 to 23.2 cm) |
| **HABITAT** | Open, sandy, gravelly, and sometimes rocky desert areas with sparse cover; from below sea level in desert sinks to about 5,000 ft. |
| **RANGE** | From southwestern New Mexico across southern Arizona to southern California and southern Nevada and tip of Utah; south through Baja, and in Sonora and Sinaloa, Mexico |
| **ALSO KNOWN AS** | *perrita* (Spanish) |

# 32 · Eastern Fence Lizard
## *Sceloporus undulatus*

Randall D. Babb

Adaptability is the key to the success of fence lizards. Across most of the U.S. and Mexico they live in forests, deserts, woodlands, flatlands, sand dunes, rocky slopes, and around buildings. Where trees are available, they are arboreal. In treeless areas, they will use rodent burrows for shelter. Their name comes from their habit of sunning on wooden fences, wood piles, or tree trunks.

The scale colors of eastern fence lizards are as variable as their living quarters. Lizards in sandy areas will have light-colored scales, for example—fence lizards depend on cryptic coloration to hide from predators. Other colors include brown, reddish, and nearly black. Crossbars, crescents, or lengthwise stripes might also be present, but sometimes not.

Although eastern fence lizards often perch on high vantage points such as fences or trees so they have a good view of approaching predators, they forage on the ground. They are sit-and-wait predators and will eat flies, grasshoppers, termites, beetles, spiders, and other arthropods. Fence lizards are also favorite prey of their larger relatives the spiny lizards, and whipsnakes.

In the Southwest, eastern fence lizards can be active all year; they breed in spring and summer. Males have two blue throat patches, while females usually lack them.

| | |
|---|---|
| **SIZE** | 3-1/2 to 7-1/2 in. (9 to 19 cm) |
| **HABITAT** | Deserts, woodlands, forests, and urban areas; from sea level to about 10,000 ft. |
| **RANGE** | In the Southwest, most of Arizona except southwestern corner, all of New Mexico and Texas; also, north to southern North Dakota, most of Colorado and Utah; in northern Mexico's Chihuahuan Desert, and east across Gulf Coast, Florida, and up to southeastern New York |
| **ALSO KNOWN AS** | Prairie lizard, plateau lizard, swift lizard |

# 33 · Desert Spiny Lizard
## *Sceloporus magister*

| | |
|---|---|
| **SIZE** | 7 to 12 in. (17.8 to 30.5 cm) |
| **HABITAT** | Desert and desert grassland plains and lower foothills, also into lower juniper woodlands; from sea level to about 5,000 ft. |
| **RANGE** | Southern California east to western Texas, south into Mexico to northwestern Sinaloa and southwestern Coahuila; also northwestern Nevada and southern Utah to tip of Baja |
| **ALSO KNOWN AS** | *Cachorón* (Spanish) |

C. Allan Morgan

The stout desert spiny lizards are notoriously bold and feisty—researchers who handle them report painful bites. Spiny lizards aggressively defend territories and will chase off intruders—even putting on a show toward humans. Smaller adversaries such as other lizards, if unlucky, might be eaten.

The four spiny lizards in the Southwest—desert, Clark's, crevice, and mountain—all have distinctive diamond-shaped spiny-looking scales on their backs. Desert spiny lizards are light-colored, usually gray, and have conspicuous black wedge-shaped patches on each shoulder. Males have blue patches on their bellies and throats, and sometimes a purple patch on their backs. When breeding in spring, females might develop reddish or orange heads.

Desert spiny lizards live in a wide range of desert habitats, as well as along washes and rivers. Often they will take shelter in the large stick-nests of packrats. Desert spiny lizards are omnivorous, foraging on insects, other lizards, flowers, fruit, and leaves.

# *34* · Tree Lizard
## *Urosaurus ornatus*

| | |
|---|---|
| **SIZE** | 4-1/2 to 6-1/4 in. (11.4 to 15.9 cm) |
| **HABITAT** | Deserts to oak and juniper woodlands, as well as along watercourses and washes; from sea level to about 9,000 ft. |
| **RANGE** | From lower Colorado River east to central Texas; from southwestern Wyoming to southern Sinaloa and northern Coahuila, Mexico |
| **ALSO KNOWN AS** | *Cachora* (Spanish) |

You often hear tree lizards before you see them. As you pass by a mesquite tree in the Southwest, listen for the quick, scratchy sound of their claws on the bark as they dart to the other side of a branch. If you move slowly around to find them, don't be surprised if you still can't see them—they're well camouflaged on the dark bark.

Tree lizards are common throughout the Southwest, from deserts up to juniper and pine-oak woodlands. Like a number of small lizards—under five inches—they are active throughout the year. During summer, they actively regulate their body temperature by moving often from shade to sun to shade. Although they prefer trees, they also live on rocks, especially in New Mexico. They hunt for small arthropods, including aphids, thrips, plant lice, beetles, bugs, flies, ants, termites, and spiders.

Male tree lizards are very territorial, and during breeding season they may sport green, yellow, orange, blue, or a combination of these colors on throat patches. They can extend these patches like little flags to add flash to their breeding displays. Females also have colored throat patches that change from light orange or yellow to vivid orange during breeding. Throughout the year males have blue bellies, while females do not.

Art Evans

# 35 · Side-blotched Lizard
## *Uta stansburiana*

Randall D. Babb

If the weather is warm, side-blotched lizards can be active any month of the year. On summer mornings they have been seen when the ground temperature is well over 110 degrees Fahrenheit. They avoid overheating by staying in the shade of small shrubs or running quickly between them as they hunt for a wide range of arthropods.

A very common lizard in the lowlands of the Southwest, the side-blotched lizard is absent only in high-elevation areas of Arizona and New Mexico. Its background color may vary, but the single dark blotch just behind each foreleg is usually easy to spot.

Males can have a home range of up to 2,500 square yards (equivalent to a square about 150 feet on each side), the borders of which they patrol to keep out other males, especially during the spring-summer breeding season. Females lay up to three clutches of eggs in a single year, depending on conditions; each clutch contains two to five eggs.

| | |
|---|---|
| **SIZE** | 4 to 6-1/4 in. (10 to 16 cm) |
| **HABITAT** | Mostly low-lying deserts and desert grassland, especially with small shrubs; sea level to about 6,000 ft. |
| **RANGE** | Throughout lower elevations of Arizona and New Mexico; lowlands of western states north to Washington; Baja, Sonora, and north-central Mexico |

# 36 · Regal Horned Lizard
## *Phrynosoma solare*

George H. H. Huey

Old desert hands still refer to horned lizards as "horny toads," knowing full well they're not toads at all. They are peculiar, though, with a flattened body and a head partially ringed with fierce-looking spikes. Enlarge one a few hundred times and you'd have a perfect star for an old B-movie—in fact, it was done; watch the 1960 classic *The Lost World*.

In real life, horned lizards are docile, but when threatened by a predator such as a fox, some horned lizards have the bizarre ability to squirt blood from a gland on each lower eyelid. The stream can reach up to four feet, and is apparently extremely distasteful to canines. Those head spikes are another defense and can even prove fatal to snakes that try to swallow a horned lizard.

Regal horned lizards are very common in the deserts of southern Arizona. Their diet is almost entirely made up of ants, which they lick up by the dozen with their sticky tongues.

A similar species, the short-horned lizard, occurs throughout eastern and northern Arizona and most of New Mexico.

| | |
|---|---|
| **SIZE** | 3-1/2 to 6-1/2 in. (8.8 to 16.6 cm) |
| **HABITAT** | Deserts and desert grasslands; from sea level to about 4,800 ft. |
| **SIZE** | Central and south-central Arizona; south through Sonora, Mexico |
| **ALSO KNOWN AS** | *Camaleón* (Spanish) |

# 37 · Great Plains Skink
## *Eumeces obsoletus*

| | |
|---|---|
| **SIZE** | 6-1/2 to 13 in. (16.5 to 34 cm) |
| **HABITAT** | In moist areas in deserts, desert grasslands, oak woodlands, and forests, especially along rivers, streams, ponds, or springs; near sea level to about 8,700 ft. |
| **RANGE** | Central and southeastern Arizona; most of New Mexico; western Texas north through Oklahoma, Kansas, and southern Nebraska |

With their shiny skin, scrawny legs, and fondness for water, skinks hardly measure up to our image of southwestern lizards. But skinks, unlike most other lizards, specialize in habitats that are moist, and they rely on stealth rather than speed for protection from predators. They live along canyon streams or in river valleys, and in moist oases in deserts, grasslands, and forests. Under cover of fallen leaves, rocks, and debris, they hunt out insects, favorites of the Great Plains skink being grasshoppers and caterpillars.

The Great Plains skink is the largest of fifteen North American skink species, at up to thirteen inches in length. It is found throughout New Mexico and in a broad swath across central and southwestern Arizona—but always in what scientists call a "mesic microclimate"; that is, a relatively damp area. The females lay a clutch of up to twenty-four eggs in late spring, which they guard during the entire two-month incubation period.

Adult Great Plains skinks normally show a clear pattern of light and dark spots on the back. The scale rows on the sides run diagonally to the back scales, unlike any other skink.

Juvenile Great Plains skinks, like several other skinks, have bright blue tails that fade with age.

Randall D. Babb

# *38* · Desert Grassland Whiptail Lizard
## *Cnemidophorus uniparens*

The old stories about an all-female race living in the Amazon made great Saturday matinee material. Sometimes nature can be just as intriguing. Eight of the Southwest's thirteen whiptail lizard species are all-female. They produce viable eggs without the need for fertilization by sperm. The young that develop in this *parthenogenic* reproduction (meaning literally "virgin birth") are exact genetic duplicates of the parent.

Whiptails are slender but long lizards—about ten inches average, two-thirds of which is a tapered tail—with thick necks and strong hind legs. Most whiptails are either obviously striped or spotted.

Whiptails hunt in open areas with jerky stop-and-go movements. They cock their heads side to side as though listening intently, and often "taste" the air with their thin, forked tongues. When a whiptail hears or smells prey—

Phil Rosen

arthropods or small lizards—it will dig furiously in loose dirt or through leaf litter to locate its meal. An area where whiptails frequently hunt will be pocked with scratch marks and craters.

The all-female desert grassland whiptail is dark brown with six or seven pale stripes running down its back, and a greenish-olive to blue-green tail. These whiptails inhabit desert grasslands and sometimes mountain canyons.

| | |
|---|---|
| **SIZE** | 6-1/2 to 10 in. (16.5 to 23.8 cm) |
| **HABITAT** | Desert grasslands, especially with mesquites, sometimes oak woodland; 3,500 ft. to about 5,000 ft. |
| **RANGE** | From central Arizona east below the Mogollon Rim, down the Rio Grande Valley to El Paso; south into northern Chihuahua, Mexico |
| **ALSO KNOWN AS** | *Huico* (Spanish) |

# 39 · Madrean Alligator Lizard
## *Elgaria kingi*

| | |
|---|---|
| **SIZE** | 7-1/2 to 12-1/2 in. (19 to 31.7 cm) |
| **HABITAT** | Near permanent water or in moist microhabitats in grasslands, oak or pine-oak woodlands, and mountain canyons; from 2,400 ft. to about 9,000 ft. |
| **RANGE** | Arizona south and east of the Mogollon Rim, southwestern New Mexico, and south into Mexico in the Sierra Madre to Jalisco |
| **ALSO KNOWN AS** | *Dragoncito* (Spanish) |

With their ten-inch bodies and tiny limbs, alligator lizards might be mistaken for snakes at first glance. They are members of the Anguid lizard family, which includes legless lizards. Anguids have heavily armored skin and very stiff bodies. The skin is so inflexible that along their sides they have rows of soft scales that act like bellows when they breathe.

Madrean alligator lizards are perfectly camouflaged for the oak woodlands and moist mountain canyons where they live in the Southwest. Their bodies are brown, marked with wavy pale gray crossbars on their backs. They have conspicuous black and white spots on their upper jaws. Their tails, which are often longer than their bodies, break off easily if they are attacked. Look or listen for alligator lizards foraging in leaf litter under trees and shrubs. They hunt for scorpions and other arthropods throughout the day, although they also venture out occasionally at night.

# TURTLES

DESERT TORTOISE

TURTLES ROUND OUT THE REPTILE FAMILIES IN NORTH AMERICA.
In the Southwest, there are two groups: freshwater turtles and land tortoises.

All freshwater turtles and land tortoises have protective shells, clawed and/or webbed feet, and horny beaks, which they use to crunch arthropods and small fish or to tear plants. Most turtles are opportunistic omnivores—they will eat plants or animals, generally whatever is most available. Some turtles are also carrion feeders.

Female turtles and land tortoises dig nests in which they lay eggs. Like all reptiles, baby turtles and tortoises are precocial, or self-reliant, when they hatch.

# 40 · Sonoran Mud Turtle
## *Kinosternon sonoriense*

| | |
|---|---|
| **SIZE** | 3-1/8 to 6-1/2 in. (8 to 16 cm) |
| **HABITAT** | Streams and ponds from deserts and desert grasslands to oak and juniper-piñon woodlands to coniferous forests; from near sea level to 6,700 ft. |
| **RANGE** | Central Arizona south to Durango, Mexico; western Texas to southeastern California |
| **ALSO KNOWN AS** | Stinkpot; *tortuga del rio* (Spanish) |

Sonoran mud turtles are amazing survivors in a region where water is often in short supply. During times of drought, such as May and June, you might see a dozen or more in one shrinking *tinaja*—a natural desert waterhole—or an intermittent mountain creek. Sonoran mud turtles can withstand high temperatures in shallow ponds that heat up in summer, and they can hibernate through cold winters by burrowing into the mud—hence their name.

All members of the mud and musk turtle family have two pairs of musk glands under the edges of their shells. They produce a strong-smelling secretion to deter predators. Mud turtles also avoid predators by remaining hidden much of the time. Their mud-colored shells are good camouflage, but you can spot them if you look carefully in calm pools where they bask with their shells barely protruding above water. The males of this small species have dark heads with creamy mottling and stripes extending back from each eye; females have plain heads.

Mud turtles slowly search the bottoms of ponds or streams for snails, and insects and their larvae, as well as small fish and tadpoles. Like all turtles, they must periodically surface for air, and how often depends on water temperature: less in cold water, more in warm. Look for mud turtles feeding during the day in spring or fall, and at night during the hottest summer months.

# 41 · Western Box Turtle
## *Terrapene ornata*

Randall D. Babb

This beautiful terrestrial turtle has such an elaborately patterned yellow and dark brown or black shell that it's often called the ornate box turtle. A small turtle with a highly domed shell, the western box prefers grassy plains and rolling hills, where it searches out beetles and other insects, as well as berries, new plant shoots, leaves, and carrion. In cattle country in the Southwest, if you see cow dung that has been torn apart, it probably means a box turtle was searching for beetles.

Look for western box turtles on roads after monsoon rains, and in grassy areas with non-rocky soil, where they dig their burrows or enlarge the existing subterranean homes of kangaroo rats or ground squirrels. Box turtles bask in the sun before foraging. From noon until late afternoon they tend to retreat to their burrows or under thick vegetation. Like other terrestrial turtles, western box turtles mate soon after emerging from hibernation in spring, and lay their eggs from about May to July.

When approached, western box turtles pull rapidly into their shell; the front of their underplate, called a plastron, is hinged so they can entirely seal off their head. When handled, these turtles are known to urinate copiously as well as bite.

| | |
|---|---|
| **SIZE** | 4 to 5-3/4 in. (10 to 15 cm) |
| **HABITAT** | Grasslands to open oak woodlands; near sea level to 6,600 ft. |
| **RANGE** | From the Midwest south to Gulf Coast; from eastern Texas across southern New Mexico to south-central Arizona; south into Sonora and Chihuahua, Mexico |
| **ALSO KNOWN AS** | Ornate box turtle; *tortuga de caja* (Spanish) |

# 42 · Desert Tortoise
## Gopherus agassizii

| | |
|---|---|
| **SIZE** | 8 to 15 in. (20 to 36 cm) |
| **HABITAT** | Deserts; in southern Arizona, rocky well-vegetated slopes and washes; in southern California and western Arizona, creosote-dominated flats |
| **RANGE** | Southern and western Arizona, far southeastern California, western Utah, southern Utah, and Sonora, Mexico; some individuals reported in southwestern New Mexico |
| **ALSO KNOWN AS** | *Tortuga del desierto* (Spanish) |

The largest native land turtle in North America, a desert tortoise can grow to more than a foot long and weigh up to nine pounds.

Desert tortoises live forty-five to fifty years or more, not straying much from home ranges a few miles square. They eat leaves, cacti, and grasses on the rocky desert slopes where they live, and they can get all the water they need from their food, although they will drink if the opportunity arises.

Their large forelegs have strong claws, which they use to dig burrows up to thirty feet long. Tortoises use burrows as retreats from midday heat and for winter hibernation. In some areas many tortoises will hibernate in one burrow.

Female tortoises dig deep crescent-shaped holes in which they lay up to fourteen eggs. When they emerge from their shells, the two-inch hatchlings must dig to the surface.

Some scientists consider the Mojave Desert populations of desert tortoises—those north and west of the Colorado River—to be biologically distinct from Sonoran Desert populations. The Mojave tortoise has declined rapidly in the last decade because of off-road vehicles and disease, among other factors, and they have been listed as threatened in the United States.

Jonathan Hanson

# FROGS, TOADS & SALAMANDERS

CANYON TREE FROG

AMPHIBIANS SUCH AS FROGS, TOADS, AND SALAMANDERS RELY ON
water for at least part of their life cycles, so in the Southwest amphibians live near wet
habitats such as lakes, creeks, cattle ponds, even golf courses with water hazards.
Amphibians have primitive lungs; to compensate, their skin absorbs oxygen as well,
but to do so the skin must always be moist. Frogs and toads are vocal and voracious
amphibians; they eat large quantities of arthropods, although some will eat other
amphibians, reptiles, small mammals, and birds.

Frogs and toads look superficially alike—they have four legs, no tail, and hop or
walk to get around—but they belong to different families. In general, frogs have
somewhat smooth skin that is damp to the touch. Usually, frogs are more aquatic than
toads. They live in or right near water, where they feed and mate.

Toads have drier skin that is warty and rough. Many toads, such as the spadefoots,
are highly resistant to dryness. They can survive without permanent water by burying
themselves underground in self-made cocoons. Protected from the dryness and cold,
the toads estivate—which is dry season dormancy, like hibernation—until water
returns with seasonal rains.

Both toads and frogs "sing" during mating season, usually spring through summer
in the Southwest. In desert areas, the July-August monsoon season is peak breeding
season. Sometimes many males will sing—croaks, trills, squawks, and toots—in group
choruses to attract females.

Frogs and toads lay eggs in the water where they develop first into swimming larvae called tadpoles, then into miniature versions of adults. They lay many thousands of
eggs so that some can survive the tremendous predation by other amphibians, reptiles,
birds, and arthropods.

# 43 · Couch's Spadefoot Toad
## *Scaphiopus couchii*

| | |
|---|---|
| **SIZE** | 1-1/4 to 3-1/2 in. (5.6 to 8.7 cm) |
| **HABITAT** | Deserts to desert grasslands, and tropical deciduous forest (Mexico); near sea level to about 5,600 ft. |
| **RANGE** | From southwestern Oklahoma across central New Mexico and Arizona; south into Baja and Sonora, Mexico |
| **ALSO KNOWN AS** | Desert spadefoot; *sapo con espuelas* (Spanish) |

Spadefoot toads are among the desert's most amazing creatures. Highly adapted to the boom-and-bust seasons of the arid Southwest, these toads emerge from underground "tombs" only after the summer rains arrive; then they participate in a raucous frenzy of mass reproduction that they must complete before the rain puddles of July and August evaporate.

To keep up their energy, spadefoot toads consume huge amounts of insects—one was observed eating fifty-five percent of its body weight in termites in a single feeding. Some scientists estimate that a Couch's spadefoot toad can eat enough at one meal to last it an entire year.

Spadefoot toads burrow into the earth using horny "spades" on their hind feet. They survive underground by shutting down their body functions almost completely; their skin dries out and hardens, creating a moisture-retaining shell.

Spadefoot eggs hatch into tadpoles within twelve to twenty-four hours; in forty-eight to seventy-two hours the tadpoles are transforming; by eleven days, fully formed adults emerge. Then, as the pools dry up, the adults bury themselves to wait until next year's rainy season.

Couch's spadefoot toad is most common in the southern arid regions of the Southwest. Its voice is a plaintive cry, somewhat sheep-like, each call lasting about a second, and its sickle-shaped spades differentiate it from the two other southwestern spadefoots.

Cecil R. Schwalbe

# 44 · Sonoran Desert Toad
## *Bufo alvarius*

Formerly known as the Colorado River toad, this large amphibian is the summertime bane of many pets in the desert Southwest—the poison secreted by its warts and glands can make a dog or cat seriously ill. If a pet bites a Sonoran Desert toad, the best remedy is a thorough mouth-rinse and a vet visit.

Sonoran Desert toads have brown or olive backs, conspicuous kidney-shaped parotid glands behind their eyes, and large warts on smooth hind legs. For such a large toad—up to seven inches long—its call is surprisingly small, like a soft ferryboat whistle, with each "blast" lasting about a half to one second.

Like most toads, Sonoran Desert toads are active at night. Their breeding season extends from about June to August, which is when you're most likely to hear them around permanent water or temporary rain pools throughout the lowland deserts and desert grasslands. After a heavy summer rain, you may see dozens of them hopping on or beside rural roads at night.

| | |
|---|---|
| **SIZE** | 4 to 7-1/2 in. (10 to 19 cm.) |
| **HABITAT** | Deserts to desert grasslands, sometimes low mountain canyons; from below sea level in low-desert sinks to about 5,300 ft. |
| **RANGE** | Southern Arizona below the Mogollon Rim east to southeastern New Mexico; south to northwestern Sinaloa, Mexico |
| **ALSO KNOWN AS** | Colorado River toad; *sapo gigante* (Spanish) |

# 45 · Woodhouse Toad
## *Bufo woodhouseii*

| | |
|---|---|
| **SIZE** | 2-1/2 to 5 in. (6 to 12.5 cm) |
| **HABITAT** | Quiet water from deserts to desert grasslands, sagebrush flats to coniferous forest valleys, as well as farms and urban areas; about sea level to 8,500 ft. |
| **RANGE** | Throughout most of the U.S. and south into Mexico to Durango; not along the Pacific Coast, western Great Lakes, or parts of Great Plains |
| **ALSO KNOWN AS** | Rocky Mountain toad |

This widespread, delicately patterned, yellowish green to brown toad is often seen at night under lights, where it catches great quantities of insects. One researcher noted a Woodhouse toad consuming two-thirds its body weight in one sitting.

Large compared to many other toads, Woodhouse toads are common in areas where there is sandy soil and adequate water for breeding—ponds, streams, irrigation ditches, backyard water holes.

Woodhouse toads breed from March to July, occasionally as late as September. One herpetologist described the male's call as sounding "like the bleating of a sheep with a cold."

# 46 · Red-spotted Toad
## *Bufo punctatus*

| | |
|---|---|
| **SIZE** | 1-1/2 to 3 in. (3.7 to 7.5 cm) |
| **HABITAT** | Rocky streams, foothills canyons, and moist arroyos from deserts to desert grasslands up to oak woodlands; from below sea level (in Death Valley) to 6,500 ft. |
| **RANGE** | Most of the Southwest and into Mexico, south throughout the Sierra Madres |

The diminutive red-spotted toad lives up to its name: its light gray to olive skin is dotted with little reddish warts. From March through September, it is an abundant member of desert, grassland, and oak woodland creek and pond communities. After summer rains begin in the Southwest, red-spotted toads are especially visible day and night crossing trails and roads. Like many toads, they feast on beetles, bees, bugs, ants, and other arthropods.

Agile rock climbers, male red-spotted toads prefer to perform their mating songs from atop exposed boulders or rocks in water or near water's edge, although some males will sing while sitting in shallow water. Their call is distinctive: a sustained-pitch long trill that is reminiscent of intermittent cricket song.

If you don't chance upon some red-spotted toads on a post-summer-rain hike in foothill canyons, try looking around large flat rocks near rocky streams or ponds.

C. Allan Morgan

# 47 · Canyon Treefrog
## *Hyla arenicolor*

Robert & Linda Mitchell

From March through August, the loud rivet-gun-like blasts of mating canyon treefrogs fill the evening air of many low-to-mid-elevation canyons and arroyos in the Southwest. These little noisemakers are surprisingly hard to see, however, because they readily flee or hide to avoid predators. If you do find them, they will likely be crouched in pockets on rocks near water—close enough to jump in if danger approaches—because despite their name they don't often climb trees.

An interesting trick of many treefrogs is their ability to change skin color rapidly, an on-demand camouflage wardrobe that is effective whether they are basking on gray granite one day or reddish rhyolite the next.

Canyon treefrogs are cream, brown, or olive-gray with dark brown or olive splotches, while their relatives the mountain treefrogs (*Hyla eximia*), Arizona's state amphibian, are green to greenish-brown, with dark eye-stripes that extend down the shoulders.

Mountain treefrogs prefer mountain meadows above about five thousand feet and call during breeding season from June to August, mostly along the Mogollon Rim and in southeastern Arizona.

| | |
|---|---|
| **SIZE** | 1-1/4 to 2-1/4 in. (3.1 to 5.6 cm) |
| **HABITAT** | Quiet pools and streams in desert grasslands up to pine-oak and piñon-juniper woodlands, and tropical thorn forests (in Mexico) |
| **RANGE** | Western Colorado and southern Utah south throughout most of Arizona and western New Mexico to northern Oaxaca, Mexico; a few populations in western Texas and the upper Pecos River in New Mexico; sea level to approx. 9,800 ft. |
| **ALSO KNOWN AS** | *Rana de arbol, rana arboricola* (Spanish) |

# 48 · Lowland Leopard Frog
## *Rana yavapaiensis*

Cecil R. Schwalbe

There are five species of leopard frogs in the Southwest, and they can be very hard to differentiate as well as to get a good look at—leopard frogs are quick to dive for cover. All have the namesake spotted backs, striped hind legs, and webbed hind feet.

Lowland leopard frogs, like all leopard frogs, live in or near mostly permanent water, even cattle ponds in desert habitats. They prefer deep water, into which they can retreat from predators such as coatimundis or coyotes; they also like debris piles in which to hide. Leopard frogs eat a variety of insects and other invertebrates.

Leopard frogs' voices are snore-like, interspersed with grunting and chuckling. Frog choruses are a medley of grunting and moaning that has been described as sounding like rubbing a thumb over a balloon. Lowland leopard frog calls are short, about half a second. The best time to observe them is during their mating seasons, from February to April, and in fall, usually October; or at night after heavy rains when they might migrate between water sources.

| | |
|---|---|
| **SIZE** | 2 to 5-2/5 in. (5 to 13.5 cm) |
| **HABITAT** | Deserts and desert grasslands to oak and pine-oak woodlands, near deep, permanent water; from near sea level to 4,800 ft., but usually below 3,300 ft. |
| **RANGE** | Colorado River drainage, western and central Arizona south of Mogollon Rim; southwestern New Mexico; northern Sonora and northwestern Chihuahua, Mexico |

# 49 · Bullfrog
## *Rana catesbeinana*

| SIZE | 3-1/2 to 8 in. (8.7 to 20 cm) |
|---|---|
| HABITAT | Nearly all wetland habitats; from near sea level to 9,000 ft. (in Colorado) |
| RANGE | Eastern U.S. to eastern Colorado and eastern New Mexico; parts of Pacific Coast; southern Canada to northeastern Mexico |

This largest of North American frogs is native east of the Rockies and came to the West and Southwest early this century with the help of game managers who thought it would make good sport and eating.

But our appetite for frog legs is far exceeded by the bullfrog's appetite for other frogs and toads, a diet that is causing local extinction of some native species such as the threatened lowland leopard frog in the Southwest. Also, because bullfrogs have few natural predators in the Southwest, some scientists estimate that their populations can reach densities ten times greater than in their native range in the East.

The bullfrog is easily recognized by its large size—up to eight inches long, sometimes well over a pound—and its olive-brown, warty, and sometimes splotchy skin. Males have a pale- to bright-yellow throat, which is equipped with an expanding vocal pouch. Their voice is described as a deeply pitched bellow (*"jug-o-rum!"*), while their alarm call is a squawk or catlike meow.

Bullfrogs live their whole lives in or very near permanent water, especially with thick vegetation such as cattails. They are sit-and-wait predators and will eat nearly anything they can swallow—insects, snails, crawfish, frogs, lizards, birds, rodents. One researcher reported a bullfrog swallowing a rattlesnake.

The best time to see bullfrogs is at night, when they "hunt" by sitting at water's edge and during breeding season, February through July, when males call loudly.

C. Allan Morgan

# 50 · Tiger Salamander
## *Ambystoma tigrinum*

Of the three species of salamanders found in the Southwest, the tiger salamander is the largest and most widespread—it's also the most beautiful, with variably patterned creamy white-to-yellow bars and spots on a black background.

Tiger salamanders, like all mole salamanders, live most of their lives underground. Because they don't have claws for digging, they use burrows built by other animals such as ground squirrels and badgers, often co-habiting with the original architect. Sometimes they live in logs or under rocks. Tiger salamanders live in most south-western habitats, from deserts to spruce-fir forests and even in cities, nearly anywhere there is calm water for breeding. In desert habitats, where ponds often dry up, tiger salamanders will dig a foot or so into the mud and enter dry-season dormancy, called *estivation*, emerging only after a good rain.

The best time to see tiger salamanders is during their breeding season, when the males and females congregate at calm bodies of water. In the southern Rocky Mountain region, tiger salamanders breed spring through fall; in the desert Southwest, they breed in spring and summer or during wet and mild winters. Look for them crawling around at night, after a few days of good rain.

| | |
|---|---|
| **SIZE** | 3 to 6-1/2 in. (7.5 to 16.2 cm); possibly up to 13 in. (33 cm) |
| **HABITAT** | Deserts to spruce-fir forests, near calm water; about sea level to 12,000 ft. |
| **RANGE** | East to west across North America, and from southern Canada to Puebla, Mexico; not in Great Basin and Mojave Deserts, or most of Pacific Coast |
| **ALSO KNOWN AS** | Waterdogs (the aquatic larvae of salamanders, which are popular as fishing bait); *ajolote, salamandra* (Spanish) |

# GLOSSARY

**amphibian**: scaleless, moist-skinned, terrestrial or aquatic vertebrate such as frogs, toads, and salamanders, the larval stage of which is aquatic (with gills) but the adult stage terrestrial (with lungs)

**arthropod**: animal with an external skeleton (exoskeleton) such as scorpions, spiders, butterflies, ants, and other insects

**bajada**: a broad, slightly sloping formation at the base of a mountain, formed when two or more alluvial fans merge (alluvial fans are accumulations of weathered debris that spills out of mountain canyons)

**brumation**: cold-season dormancy; see *estivation*

**carnivore**: animal that eats other animals

**cloaca**: single opening that serves for elimination of body wastes and contains sexual organs; the outside opening of the cloaca is called the vent

**crepuscular**: active near dusk and dawn

**desiccation**: loss of body moisture

**ectodermic**: unable to internally regulate body temperature; dependent on external sources for heat

**endothermic**: can internally regulate body temperature; produces internal heat through metabolism

**estivation**: a period of reduced activity that some reptiles, amphibians, and mammals use to reduce their need for food and water during times of extreme drought and/or heat (some herpetologists use the term "brumation" to indicate cold-season dormancy)

**glottis**: the opening of a snake's trachea, which extends and acts like a snorkel in the bottom of the mouth, allowing a snake to breathe while swallowing food

**herbivore**: animal that eats plants

**herpetology, herpetologist**: the study of reptiles and amphibians; one who studies reptiles and amphibians

**omnivore**: animal that eats plants, animals, carrion—just about anything

**reptile**: scaly, dry-skinned vertebrate that has lungs and reproduces by eggs or live-born young

**riparian corridor**: a watercourse, either permanent or ephemeral; generally associated with broad-leaved trees such as cottonwood, sycamore, and walnut

**rostral**: the scale at the tip of a reptile's nose

**vent**: *see* cloaca

**vertebrate**: animal with a backbone

# SUGGESTED READING

Brown, David E., and Neil B. Carmony. 1999. *Gila Monster: Facts and Folklore of America's Aztec Lizard*. Salt Lake City: University of Utah Press.

Degenhardt, W. G., C. W. Painter, and A. H. Price. 1996. *Amphibians and Reptiles of New Mexico*. Albuquerque: University of New Mexico Press.

Ernst, Carl H. 1999. *Venomous Reptiles of North America*. Washington and London: Smithsonian Institution Press.

Greene, Harry. 1997. *Snakes—The Evolution of Mystery in Nature*. Berkeley: University of California Press.

Klauber, Laurence M. 1997. *Rattlesnakes: Their Habits, Life Histories and Influence on Mankind*. Reprinted from 1972. Berkeley: University of California Press.

Lowe, Charles H., Cecil R. Schwalbe, and Terry B. Johnson. 1986. *The Venomous Reptiles of Arizona*. Phoenix: Arizona Game and Fish Department.

Sherbrooke, Wade C. 2003. *Introduction to Horned Lizards of North America*. Berkeley: University of California Press.

Stebbins, Robert C. 1985. *A Field Guide to Western Reptiles and Amphibians*. Boston: Peterson Field Guides, Houghton Mifflin.

# INDEX